East Joins West

Chinese Astrology for Western Astrologers

Monica Hable Dimino and Paula Sherwin

ACS Publications
an imprint of Starcrafts LLC

East Joins West
Chinese Astrology for Western Astrologers

Copyright © 2016 by
Monica Hable Dimino and Paula Sherwin

ACS Publications

All rights reserved.
No part of this book may be reproduced or used in any form or by any means—graphic, electronic or mechanical, including photocopying, mimeographing, recording, taping or information storage and retrieval systems—without written permission from the publisher.
A reviewer may quote brief passages.

Text by Monica Hable Dimino and Paula Sherwin
Illustrations by Paula Sherwin

Production Design by Maria Kay Simms

International Standard Book Number
978-1-934976-65-4

Library of Congress Control Number: 201 695 0543

First printing October 2016

Published by ACS Publications
an imprint of Starcrafts LLC
68 A Fogg Rd
Epping, NH 03042

Printed in the United States of America

Monica Hable Dimino Dedication

I dedicate this book to my personal menagerie:
Paul, Philip, Isabel and Martin

Acknowledgments

This journey began over 50 years ago when Lilette Lizarralde introduced me to the Chinese symbols via Paula Delsol's inimitable book, "Horoscopes Chinois" as I was launching my own studies in Western Astrology.

I walked hand in hand with both women when an NCGR conference in Kansas City dedicated its theme of East Meets West to both traditions, and I had an opportunity to speak on this theme. Strong positive feedback after my lecture then led to an invitation to present this material at the UAC Conference in 1998 in Atlanta. Lee Lehman had made this space available to me.

Then Michael Lutin also supported my work on this theme when he invited me to lecture in New York City in 2007.

When Paula Sherwin visited me in January, 2013, she got the project of our writing about the theme into focus. It was her brilliant support and artistic contributions that kept "our" baby alive until Maria Kay Simms took over by agreeing that ACS Publications would publish our book.

My acknowledgments would not be complete without also thanking Robert Corre for his consistent encouragement, the OPA group led by Arlan Wise for their initial publication of this material in their newsletter, and ISAR's Richard and Vicky Smoot for presenting this work in their Journal in 2014. So many colleagues in our National Organizations have supported this work!

Also my students and my clients have added to my learning of the archetypes of these "animalitos" until they have become etched in my soul!

Paula Sherwin Dedication

This book is dedicated with love to the most powerful and delightful women
with whom I am honored to share my life:
My mother, Paula Sowers, a Fire Tiger with a Pisces Sun who lives life
with limitless energy and even greater compassion.
My eldest daughter, Alexis, an Earth Tiger with a Scorpio Sun
who leads the life of a passionate and beautiful warrior.
My youngest daughter, Sierra, a Wood Rooster with a Libra Sun
who generously shares her artistic qualities creating harmony and strength in her wake.
And my sister, Barbara Heward, a Wood Goat with a Libra Sun
who enjoys life with an abundance of charm, love, and humor.

Paula Sherwin Acknowledgments

I lovingly acknowledge my dear friend and astrological mentor,
Monica Hable Dimino,
whose passion and love of astrology has changed the course of my life.
Without Monica's insight and wisdom and my love of astrology,
this endeavor would never have been possible.

I would also like to thank Nancy Murdock,
who is a most astute and delightful astrologer and teacher
whose understanding and intimate relationship
with astrology fills me with awe.

Finally, with whole heart I thank my father, Clyde Sowers,
whose lifelong faith in me gave me the strength, confidence,
and determination to endeavor to be all I can be.
His belief in me continues to guide me from afar.

Table of Contents

Chinese Astrology for Western Astrologers 1
The Story of How the Animals Were Selected by the Buddha 2
The Actual History of the Zodiac 3
Features of the Lunar World in Chinese Astrology 4
The Chinese Zodiac 5
The Twelve Animal Signs and their Hours (illustration) 7
The Elements 8   Compatibility 10
Motivations of the Animals of the Zodiac 11
Differences Between Western and Eastern Astrology 13
The Humanitarian Animal Triads (illustration) 14
The Mental Animal Triads (illustration) 15
The Rat is the Midnight Animal—Motivations of the Rat . . . 16, illustration 17
The Ox, the 2nd Animal, Motivations of the Ox . . . . 18, illustration 19
The Tiger, the 3rd Animal, Motivations of the Tiger . . . . 20, illustration 21
The Rabbit, the 4th Animal . . . . 24, illustration 23
The Dragon, the 5th Animal . . . . .26, illustration 25
The Snake, the 6th Animal . . . . .28, illustration 29
The Horse, the 7th Animal . . . . .32, illustration 31
The Goat, the 8th Animal . . . . 34, illustration 33
The Monkey, the 9th Animal . . . . illustration 35, text 36
The Rooster, the 10th Animal . . . . illustration 37, text 38
The Dog, the 11th Animal . . . . illustration 39, text 40
The Pig, the 12th Animal . . . . illustration 41, text 41-42
What Next? 43
The Chinese Calendar 1937-2020 44-46
A Special Offer for an Art Print of Your Animal 47
About Monica Hable Dimino 48
About Paula Sherwin 49

Chinese Astrology for Western Astrologers

Students of the Tropical Zodiac ask, "Why clutter our Astrology with other stuff?" It's true, Western Astrology is very complex. Why would an Astrologer want to understand Chinese Astrology?

To study both systems provides a rounded whole. Let's begin by roughly describing these two systems. Chinese Astrology is based on a lunar calendar. The year in Chinese Astrology begins with the first New Moon in the Western sign of Aquarius. Like the Moon, the date fluctuates from year to year. There is a sixty year cycle in which the twelve animals show up in the elemental guises of metal, water, wood, fire, or earth. Very lunar, the elements for each animal are never the same in that sixty year cycle.

Western Astrology is solar based. It enjoys the regularity of the Sun. The twelve signs are consistent. The signs begin on predictable dates, always measured by the Sun's motion. The signs of the Zodiac also have elements associated with them (fire, earth, air, and water), but, like the Sun, these are stable designations. They are always the same for each sign.

So, we have two major frames. The Solar frame organizes the more rational side of life and the Lunar frame relates to unconscious traits. The Solar world is as dependable as night follows day. It suits the rational mind. It allows us to organize life in a practical way. The Lunar world, on the other hand, is visceral and erratic at times. It is unpredictable and sometimes seemingly devoid of logic. It keeps us connected to the ebb and flow of nature.

The Story of How the Animals Were Selected by Buddha

If there was a developmental process in defining this system, the commonly accepted story involves the Buddha. It is said that Buddha called all the animals for a race to meet him at the wisdom tree.

The tale of the race is that during the journey, the animals were involved in everything from cheating to heroism. For example the Rat, who won the race, did so through tricking the Ox. The busy Ox was ahead of the rest of the animals because Ox is so productive and he doesn't take his eyes off the goal.

However, the Rat, an animal who is very astute, clever, and very ambitious was running behind the Ox until he decided to get on the Ox's back. Just as the Ox was reaching the finish line, Rat leapt off and he won the race. The diligent Ox keeps moving and the clever Rat decides to get ahead in a different way. The Rat isn't a big animal but it can take advantage of the Ox's determination.

The Tiger was a strong swimmer, so he came in third. The Rabbit was fourth since he jumped his way across the river and was also helped by the Dragon.

By all accounts the altruistic Dragon could have won the race as it could fly. Depending on the story, the Dragon stopped for a number of reasons; to help villagers caught in a flooding river, to assist the Rabbit in the race to Buddha, as well as creating rain for farmland.

The Dragon was followed by the Horse that was carrying the Snake in its hoof. The sneaky Snake had hidden in the hoof of the Horse in order to cross the river. When they got to the other side, the Snake jumped out as they reached the shore and scared the Horse into seventh place.

The Goat, Monkey and Rooster all helped each other cross the river. The Dog would have been close to the front but decided to take a bath halfway through. Finally, the Pig reached the opposite shore after nibbling along the way, and completing the Chinese Zodiac.

The Actual History of the Zodiac

The actual history behind the Chinese Zodiac is harder to ascertain. It's known from pottery artifacts that the animals of the zodiac were popular as early as the Tang Dynasty (618-907 A.D.), but they were also seen much earlier from artifacts dating from the Warring States Period (475-221 B.C.). It's been written that the animals of the zodiac were brought to China via the Silk Road, the same central Asian trade route that brought the Buddhist belief from India to China.

But some scholars argue that the belief predates Buddhism and has origins in early Chinese astronomy that used the planet Jupiter as a constant, as its orbit around the earth took place every 12 years.

Still others have argued that the use of animals in astrology began with nomadic tribes in ancient China who developed a calendar based on the animals they used to hunt and gather.

(The above information is from "The Origins of the Chinese Zodiac—It's More Than Just a Sign" by Lisa Chiu, Journalist.)

Features of the Lunar World in Chinese Astrology

The characteristics that describe the animal years, to a great extent, do correspond to the animal psychology that we associate with these creatures.

But why, we might ask, would a native of a particular year have these basic traits? The Lunar world that we are moving in does not provide answers. Instead, it invites us to accept these ideas as givens.

Understanding Chinese Astrological animals will provide a foundation for the energy of the year you are studying. For example, if you are born in the Year of the Ox, your energy will be much more contained or throttled relative to productivity because Oxen don't like to waste time.

Oxen also dislike using a lot of words to express themselves in a dramatic way. This is true of any Ox, even in the signs that are chattier. For example, an Aries Ox would be throttled back.

This is how the energy of the Chinese Zodiac affects the signs of the Western Zodiac.

Also, because Chinese Astrology relates to the lunar, i.e., unconscious tendencies, we may not recognize or relate to these animals in ourselves. They rule our inner nature, not the nature that we analyze and attempt to understand. The Chinese animals teach us what people do unconsciously, rather than consciously, because that is "their" nature.

The Chinese Zodiac

It is important to put these animals into either a day or a night context. The top half of the chart that is shown on page 7 is day (6 am to 6 pm). High noon is at the top of the chart, 11 am to 1 pm. The bottom half of the chart is night (6 pm to 6 am). Midnight is 11 pm to 1 am, as you see at the bottom of the chart.

The chart is broken into two hour segments. These segments can be compared to Ascendant positions in Western Astrology.

Look at the animal names in each section, moving clockwise from the bottom. The Midnight animal is the Rat (the period from 11 pm to 1 am). Next is the Ox, from 1 to 3 am. Tiger's segment is 3 to 5 am. The Rabbit represents daybreak, from 5 until 7 am, which corresponds to the Ascendant position in Western charts.

Next, then, comes Dragon, from 7 to 9 am. The Snake's segment is from 9 to 11 am. At high noon we have Horse, from 11 am to 1 pm, as you see at top of the chart.

Goat begins the afternoon hours from 1 to 3 pm, followed by Monkey from 3 to 5 pm. Rooster's segment is from 5 to 7 pm, which includes sunset, and corresponds to the position of the Descendant in Western charts. Then, through the evening, we have Dog from 7 to 9 pm and then Pig from 9 to 11 pm, then we're back to the segment of the Rat again.

In Western Astrology, a majority of planetary positions can fall in the Eastern or Western side (left or right half) of the chart. People with Eastern charts are self-sufficient. They may not have as much need for other people as those with Western charts.

The same thing is true of Chinese Astrology. The Eastern animals, represented by the morning hours, are more self-reliant (Rat, Ox, Tiger, Rabbit, Dragon, and Snake). These are the signs we have the most difficulty understanding because they aren't your normal barnyard animals. We don't get a strong psychological definition for the exotic Eastern animals

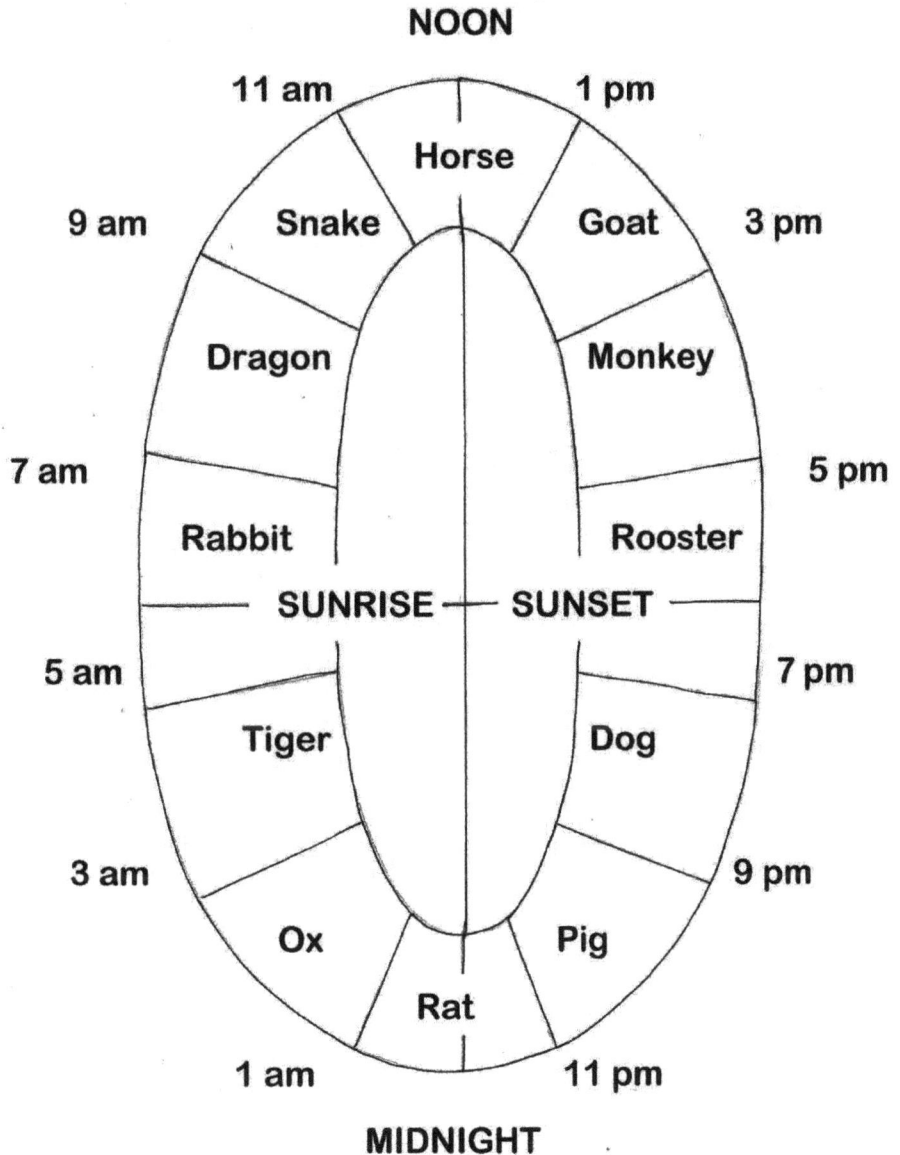

because they are independent and take care of themselves. On the Western side, we find the familiar animals. Most can be domesticated. We understand them. This is the very sociable side of this Zodiac.

Animals that are below the horizon (Rat, Ox, Tiger, Pig, and the Dog) are very private. They don't feel comfortable in the limelight. Nocturnal animals are difficult to understand because they are ruled by the Moon.

Those animals which are above the horizon (Dragon, Snake, Horse, Goat, and Monkey) are attuned to the day time world. They function well in visible positions because they understand the dependable structures of the solar world. These animals are comfortable working with clarity, transparency and things that they can demonstrate or explain to other people.

The Elements

The element of the animal year modifies the behavior of the assigned animal. Years that finish in 0 and 1 are called metal years. You have the metal Horse, metal Goat, etc. Years ending in 2 and 3 are water years. Years ending in 4 and 5 are wood years. Years ending in 6 and 7 are fire years. Years ending in 8 and 9 are earth years.

Metal years (ending in 0 and 1) are extremely strong and firm in their positions. Metal does not bend. Metal is firm; it takes charge. It feels comfortable with a certain structure. Obama is a strong metal Ox.

Water years (ending in 2 and 3) can be powerful, but subtle. Here you have Vice President Joe Biden. He is more connected to Congress than Obama will be because water is automatically empathic.

Wood years (ending in 4 and 5) could be the equivalent of air in Western Astrology. Wood is intellectual and attached to ideas and communications. Winston Churchill was a Wood Dog. He was able to handle the complexity of World War II and could thereby hold the diverse forces together often with oratory, relating the pieces to the whole.

Fire years (ending in 6 and 7) are related to keeping things moving. Fire is always inspirational. Fire sets us up to feel a desire to follow somebody. Bill Clinton was a Fire Dog. He was always getting us fired up about something. George Bush, Jr., was also a Fire Dog, launching the 21st century with dreams of tax breaks and renewed conservative power.

Earth years (ending in 8 and 9) are practical. Sometimes people have no earth planets in their charts, but if they are born in an Earth year, they can be extremely practical. People born in the earth years provide these skills. Consider Abraham Lincoln, Teddy Roosevelt, and Albert Einstein.

Frequently, people who are very humanitarian will find people who are very mental to be too logical, too rational, and perhaps lacking in empathy and humanitarian values.

Similarly, people who are very mental may feel that humanitarians are not very logical, not very scientific, and appear to not have tangible reasons for their empathic behaviors.

The same is true for the Yin or the Yang qualities. It may be easier to accept the Yin and Yang qualities of our own triads, but it may be more complex to relate the Yin and Yang of the other triads.

(Diagrams of the Yin and Yang triads are shown on pages 14 and 15.)

Compatibility

Most of the time, we feel stressed with the animal that is opposite us (six years before or after our own year). For example, Rats feel tension with Horses, Oxen with Goats, Tigers with Monkeys, Rabbits with Roosters, Dragons with Dogs, and Snakes with Pigs.

However, it shouldn't be seen as a limit when relationships go out of their comfort zone. There is compatibility between these opposites. We often look for our opposites in the Chinese Zodiac. Many Oxen are attracted to Goats. The very serious, steady Oxen seem to get emotional release from the capricious Goat.

Dragons and Dogs are often seen together. Dogs, which are so often purposeful and duty bound, can be lifted from that dogged seriousness by Dragons, who seem to trust life wherever it takes them. It all depends on how much we need to find contrast in our lives.

Some animals need the leavening of opposition and contrast, whereas other animals are very eager to find harmony in the approach of values.

There is nothing that mandates that all Dogs need to be with Dogs or Snakes with Snakes. Lives that need stability will probably be drawn to animals that are steady such as the Oxen. If you are drawn to Snakes, your destiny may be one of a very deep, metaphysical journey.

There are certain signs that have energy patterns that we need. For example, the fire years might be attracted to the air years. The Earth years might be comfortable with the Water years.

Most of the time, the combinations that work are the combinations that provide that animal with something he or she needs.

Although Chinese Astrologers consider the most important animals to be those that represent the Animal of the Year, the Hour, the Season and the Day of your birth, this book will highlight only the Animal of the Year and the Animal of your birth hour.

Motivations of the Animals of the Zodiac

Chinese animals of the Zodiac are motivated differently. Some animals are moved by the mind; others are moved by the heart.

Animals also enjoy either Yin or Yang qualities. Yang initiates action while Yin is more receptive. The pattern is as follows:

Because of these motivations and qualities, there are certain affinities between groups of animals. There is an affinity within all the mental groups as there is within all the humanitarian groups. There is also an affinity between those animals who share the same qualities (Yin or Yang).

Animals within triads have a natural empathy or natural connectedness to each other. It is easy to get on board with either of the mental signs if you have the mental component whether they are Yin or Yang. The same is true of the humanitarian signs. There is a natural sharing of values and approaches to life. The easiest relationships are formed when we are in our animal triad. Those relationships are the most compatible.

Frequently, people who are very humanitarian will find people who are very mental too logical, too rational, and perhaps lacking in empathy and humanitarian values. Similarly, people who are very mental may feel that humanitarians are not very logical, not very scientific, and appear to not have tangible reasons for their empathic behaviors.

The same is true for the Yin or the Yang qualities. It may be easier to accept the Yin and Yang qualities of our own triads, but it may be more complex to relate the Yin and Yang of the other triads.

Differences between Western and Eastern Astrology

Chinese astrology

Tends to make a statement regarding animals that suggest fate.
For instance, Rabbits are not supposed to suffer,
Horses always lead the parade, Dragons' energy holds sway,
and Serpents carry karmic destinies.

Western astrology

Tells a story. It is about traits, not fates.
It highlights solar, free will expression.

Chinese Astrology

Appears fated or predetermined.
It points to givens, not about combating these givens.

Western astrology

Suggests ways to alter the future
with the use of free will.

The Humanitarian Animal Triads

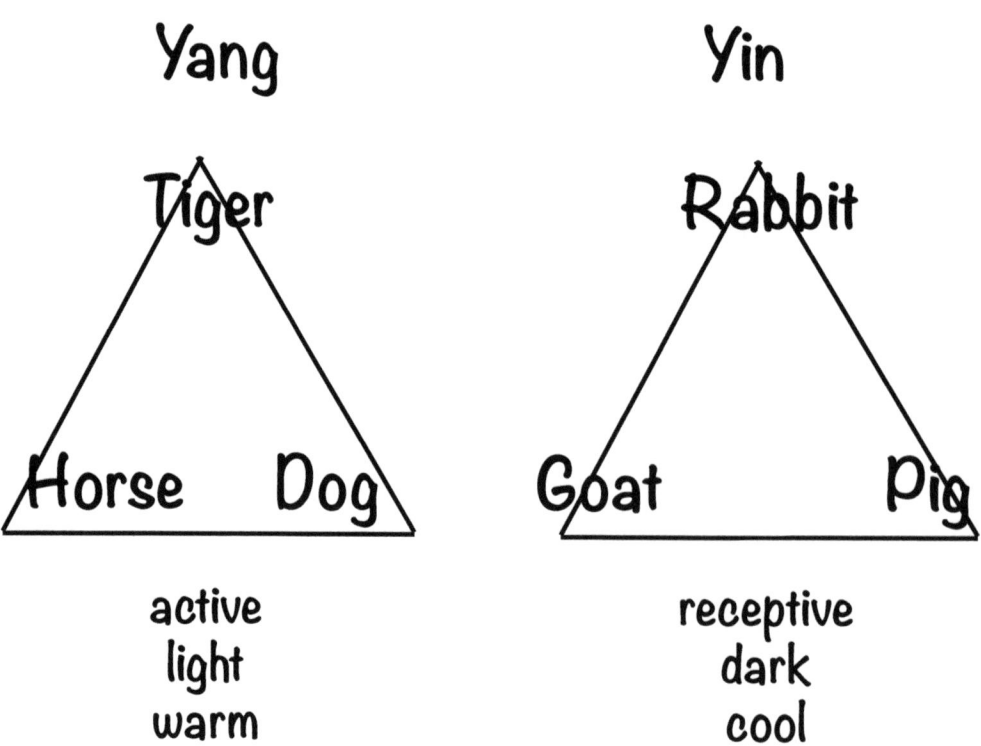

These triads have a natural sharing of empathy and connectedness.

The Mental Animal Triads

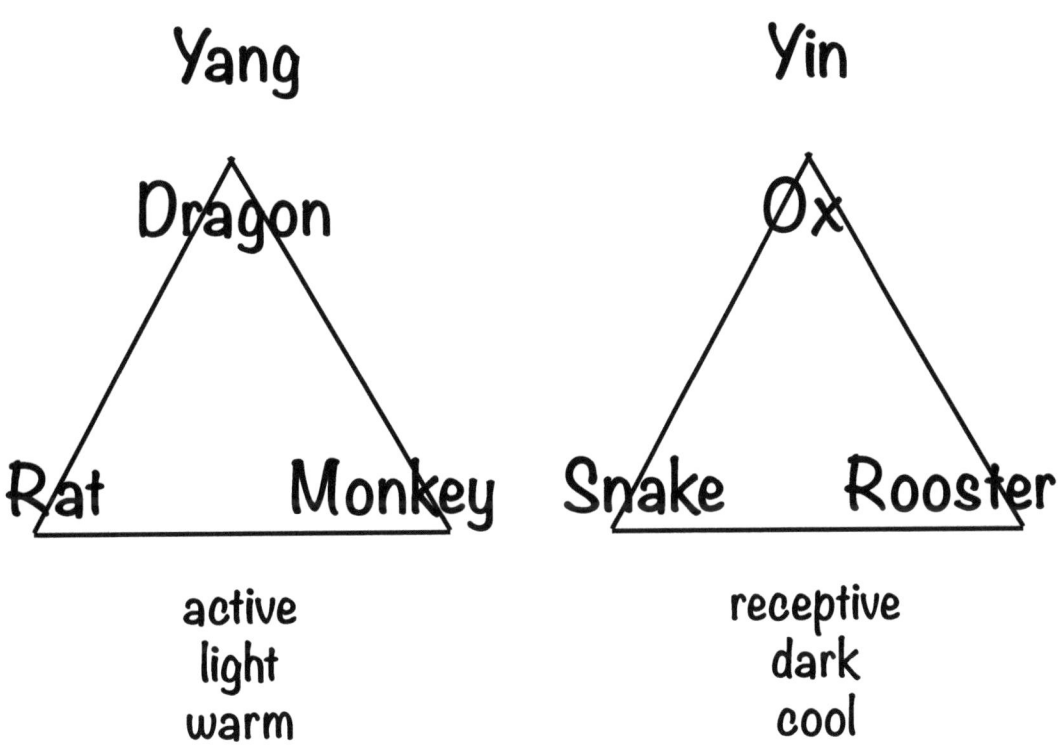

These triads have a natural sharing of logic and reason.

The Rat is the Midnight animal (11 pm to 1 am).

Rats scurry around in the dark. The Rat is the animal that most people shun, so Rats will typically have a very charming nature to compensate.

Motivations of the Rat

Charisma and a conquering spirit is very much a part of their nature. Their hidden location gives the Rat information about what is happening in the invisible, subterranean world. Those born in the Year of the Rat are not always comfortable on stage unless they are adequately disguised.

Rats prefer occupations where they are not endangered. They want to be safe to some extent. Rats make good writers, thinkers, and journalists where they can put their information out on paper. Rats will often have successful careers in one world and will earn their living by doing simple jobs like bookkeeping, tax keeping, or bureaucratic positions where it is possible to keep their identity hidden. They have rich intellectual inner lives.

Rats hate to be caught off guard and are quick to respond with aggression. TS Elliott was a Rat. A very private man, he didn't like to be photographed. His world was kept under wraps as he worked regular 9-5 jobs.

Famous Rats include:

Galileo, George Washington, Richard Nixon, Jimmy Carter, Charles, Prince of Wales, Vice President Al Gore, Lauren Bacall, Marlon Brando, Dr. Oz, and Pope Francis.

ANIMALS OF THE CHINESE ZODIAC

The first animal in the Chinese Zodiac is the Rat.

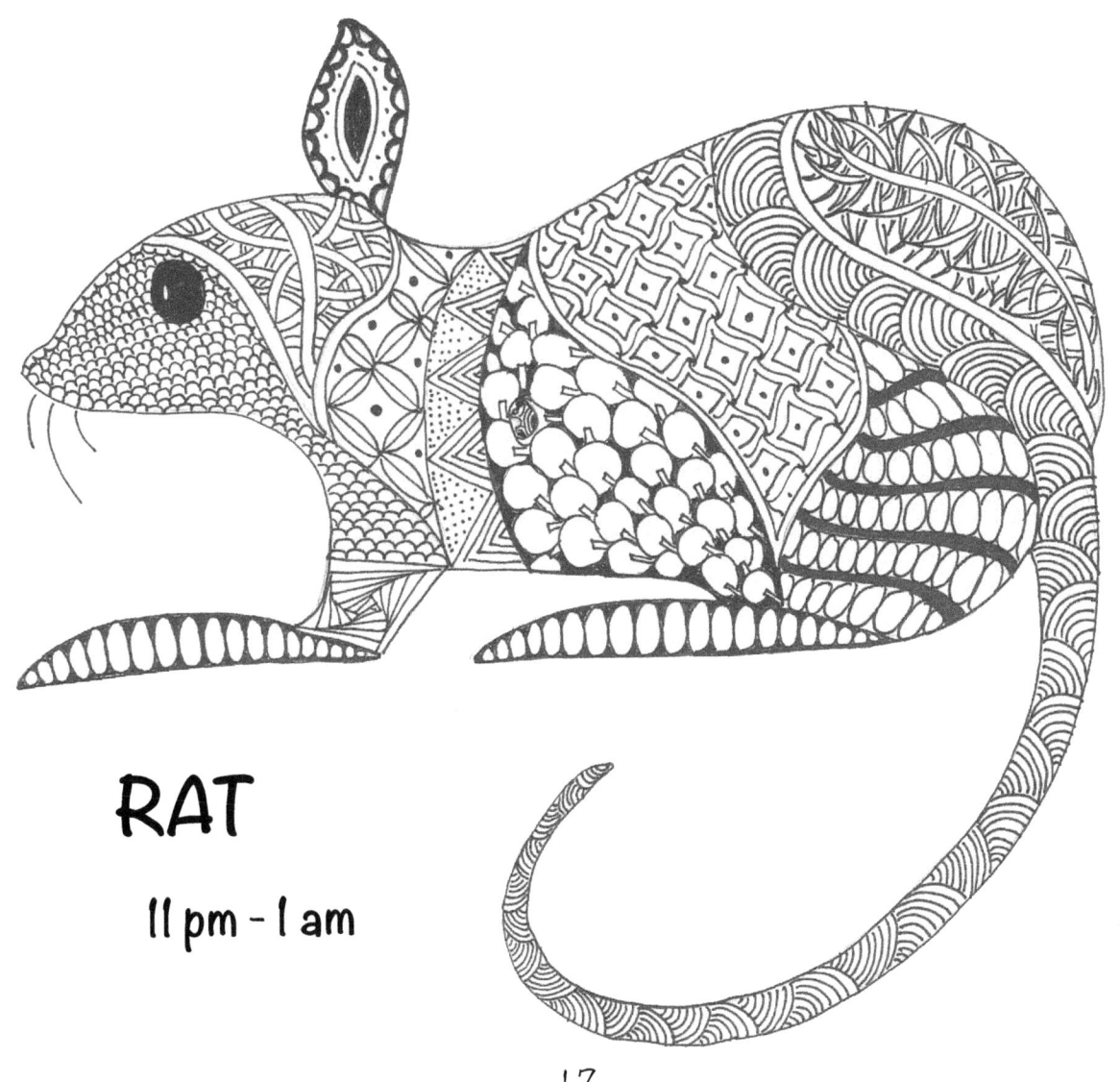

RAT

11 pm - 1 am

Motivations of the Ox

The Ox, second animal of the Chinese zodiac, also works best off stage, and represents the capacity to work efficiently, effectively and focus on a goal. An Ox is not in a hurry, but instead takes things into its own stride, is loyal, trustworthy, sturdy, and hardworking. But we don't know the innermost thoughts of Oxen because they do not reveal themselves easily. We must observe them to "see" what they are all about.

It is unusual to see an Ox without success, but this success is based on dedicated work. Oxen are not inclined to talk a lot. They expect you to know what they feel by what they do. Even in love they can be very quiet.

Oxen types are people who like to be in a family setting. They are dedicated to family, home, and country. Oxen are opaque, but we don't fear them because their work ethic gives us a sense of who they are.

Famous Oxen include:

Barack Obama and Robert F Kennedy. Robert F Kennedy is a good example of an Ox with a big, solid family. Barack Obama is a hardworking Ox who has developed a strong family center in his adult life.

Other Oxen are Charlie Chaplin, Adolf Hitler, Walt Disney, Richard Burton, Paul Newman, Johnny Carson, Margaret Thatcher, Meryl Streep, Jack Nicholson, Colin Powell, George Clooney, Robert Redford, Jeff Bridges, Eddie Murphy, , Lady Diana, and Elizabeth Warren.

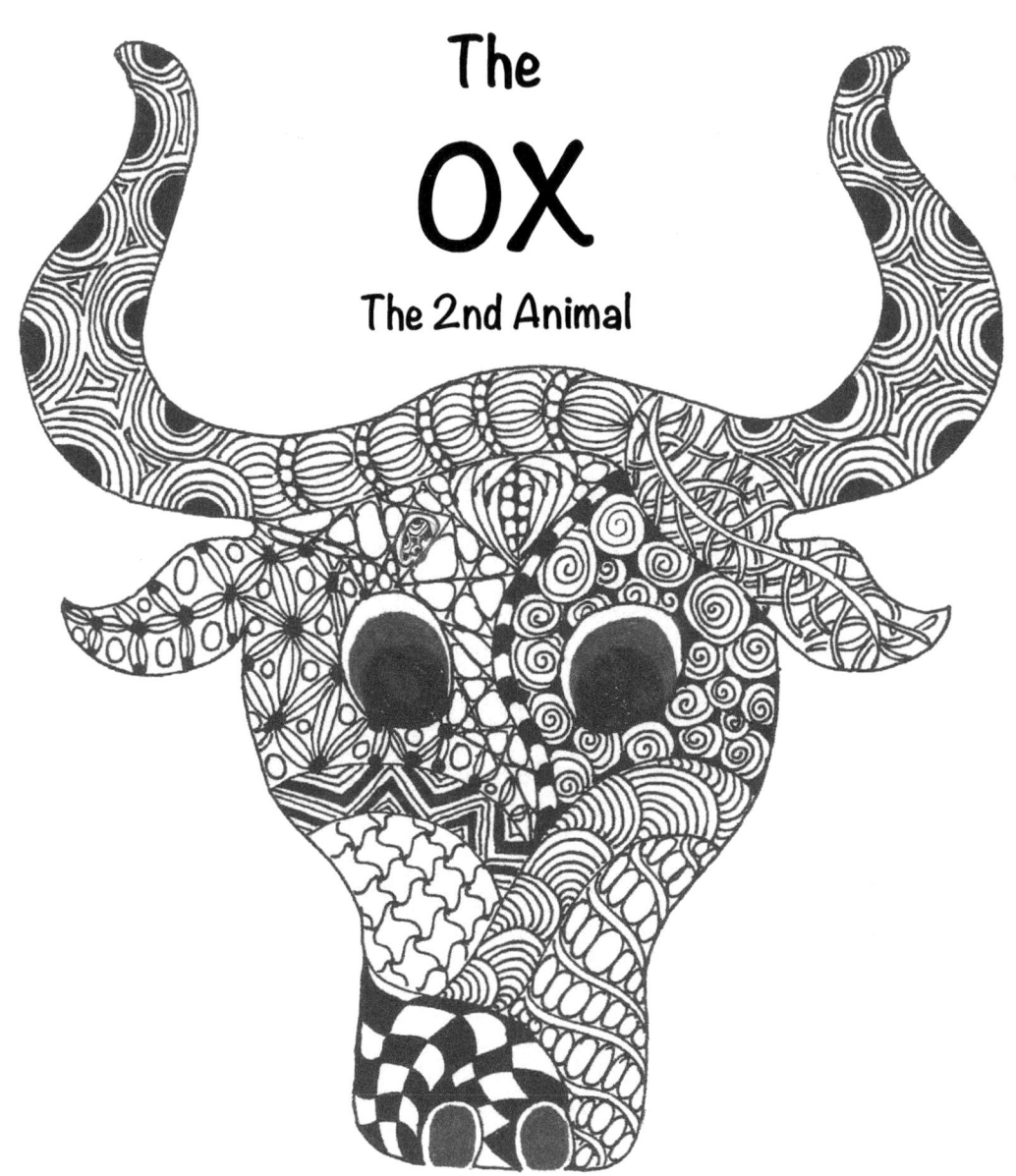

The OX
The 2nd Animal

The Ox is a night animal (1-3 am).

Motivations of the Tiger
The 3rd animal is the Tiger.

Tiger definitely works very well with a certain amount of night life. But a Tiger, like the Snake, is a jungle animal and is not well understood. The Animals on the sunrise side of the wheel cannot be understood by applying the same psychology that applies to barnyard animals that can be observed in our everyday world.

The Tiger is another animal that deeply connects with the invisible world. This connection is one which leaves him or her either very inert or hyperactive. That is the curious thing about Tigers. They are busy when they have something to do or when they are upset about something. But when that something is done, they love to spend long hours relaxing.

Another characteristic of Tigers is that they expect to be the boss. It is possible that the Ox would also like to be in charge, but the Tiger would be overt about it. The Tiger wants to get to the top and does not want to take the quiet forward motion of the Ox to do so. The Tiger is eager and impatient to reach the heights that he or she covets.

The interesting thing about Tigers is this; they often reach their destinies without planning or design. That is not to say that they are not planners, but more precisely, these are people who have reached places of importance almost by destiny.

TIGER

The Tiger is another night animal.

(3 - 5 am)

For example, Queen Elizabeth, II, is a Tiger. She was not born to be Queen of anything. Her Uncle Edward was to have his lineage honored with the crown.

But when Edward abdicated, his brother became King George, who had two daughters who were then the next in line for the crown. It was the fate of the elder daughter, Elizabeth, to become Queen Elizabeth II. She is now the longest serving monarch in British history.

Tigers sit on the fence. "Should I? Shouldn't I?" So, they are frequently plagued by doubts.

If a Tiger is unsure, that tells us that he or she has not really connected with his or her gut feelings. When a Tiger does connect, though, he or she does not sit on the fence, but acts quickly and directly.

Famous Tigers include:

Karl Marx, Charles de Gaulle, Josef Stalin,
Ho Chi Minh, John Steinbeck,
Dwight D. Eisenhower, Queen Elizabeth II,
Marilyn Monroe, Fidel Castro, Jay Leno,
William Hurt, Rudolf Nureyev,
Tom Cruise, Jodie Foster,
and Jon Stewart.

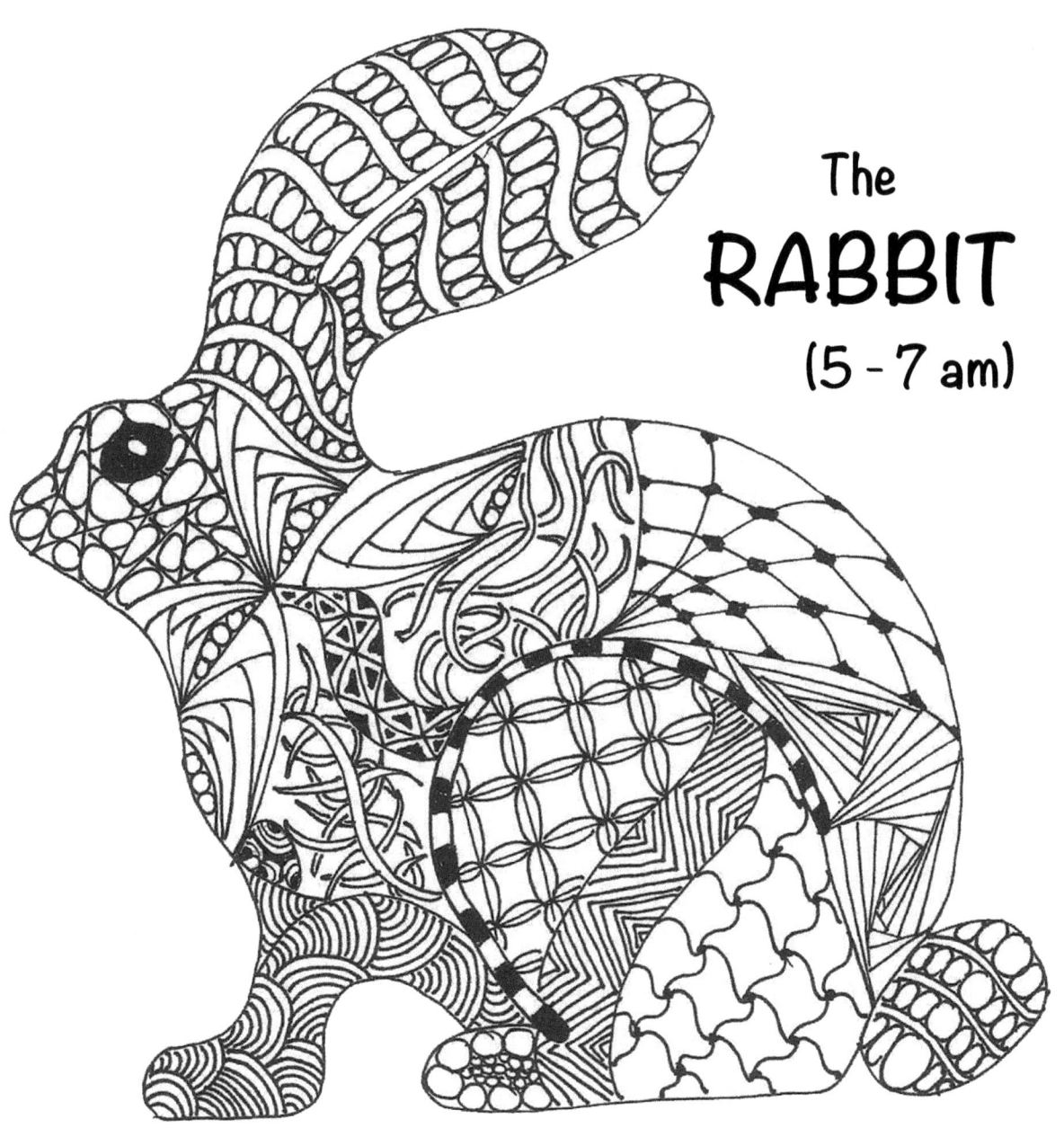

The
RABBIT
(5 - 7 am)

The 4th animal of the Chinese zodiac is the Rabbit (5 - 7 am).

The Rabbit is the Spring animal that also represents the dawning day.

Rabbits are difficult to fathom. By nature they are very cultivated, nice looking, and have a comfortable demeanor.

There is not a pugnacious quality in these lovely animals. They gravitate to success because they don't get involved with unsettling exchanges. Therefore, people born in the Year of the Rabbit can gravitate to high places primarily because they are very presentable, are never outspoken, and they typically don't make a scene.

Rabbit clients won't tell you what they want. It is not that they are being secretive like Scorpio. They are simply enigmatic. Maybe they don't know themselves what they want.

Famous Rabbits include:
Queen Victoria, Albert Einstein, Dr. Benjamin Spock, Orson Welles, David Rockefeller, Bob Hope, Frank Sinatra, Robin Williams, Johnny Depp, Nicholas Cage, Sting, Francis Ford Coppola, Michelle Obama, Brad Pitt, Angelina Jolie, and Tiger Woods.

The
DRAGON

The Dragon is often seen as the most important animal in the Chinese Zodiac (7 - 9 am).

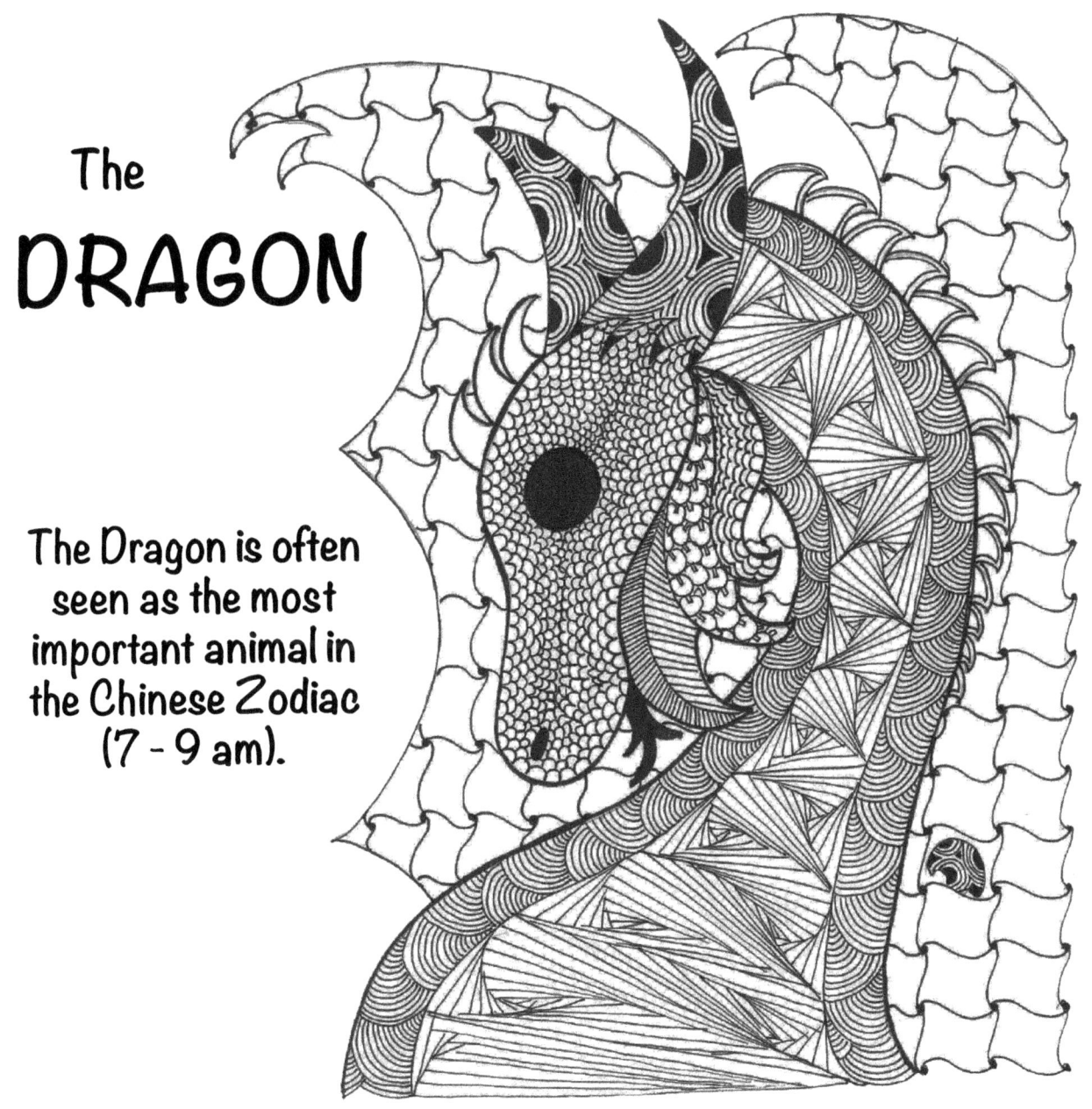

The 5th Animal is the Dragon.

All Chinese women want to give birth to Dragon children in the Dragon year. The Dragon is the only animal that is mythological because it doesn't really exist. Therefore, Asian cultures, which love Dragons, attribute lots of qualities to people born in the Dragon years. Dragons are supposed to protect against war, famine, fire, and disasters. Dragons create a feeling of safety and security.

People frequently look up to Dragons. However, the Dragon doesn't seem to have a North on its compass. This animal is all energy and known for nobility, but often Dragons don't know where to direct that energy. When asked, "Where do you want to go?" Dragons frequently have no idea. There are just too many possibilities! They need partners to direct their very special energy. Dragons frequently want to associate with others who are needed to help them to direct their incredible energy into channels of success.

For the Dragon to unleash his or her energy and trust that the outcome will be right is more significant than knowing where the energy will land. The Dragon doesn't need to have the answers, just the push to make paths possible. Vladimir Putin is a Dragon. He seems to inspire Russians with a lot of confidence. He keeps winning elections, but it is hard to know what he really wants to do with all his power.

Famous Dragons include:

St. Joan of Arc
Florence Nightingale
Sigmund Freud
J. Paul Getty
Salvadore Dali
Walter Cronkite
Martin Luther King
John Lennon
Ringo Starr
Al Pacino
Russell Crowe
Sandra Bullock

The 6th Animal is the Snake
Snakes are mystical (9 - 11 am).

They are prophetic; listen to what they say. Something they say today, whether about public events or personal stories, will be tomorrow's reality.

Snakes are sexy, sensual, and attractive. Many Snakes have affairs and are unfaithful. This infidelity isn't as seriously objectionable as one might think.

Snakes are here to heal us, help us, to enable us to handle our karma. Many people are healed in this way.

If a Snake has an affair, it is probably because he is working on the deeper levels of individuals who need certain experiences in order to be healed. JFK was a Snake. Look at all his affairs.

We can't understand Snakes. They are not part of our daily life. We only understand the Snake by its manifestations which can be psychic or startling.

We are not talking about people with ordinary lives. Snakes always bring out deeper levels and experiences in the people with whom they associate. Snake dredges the invisible world and brings it to manifestation.

Abraham Lincoln and Mao Tse-tung were Snakes and both were subtle leaders.

The SNAKE

Other famous Snakes include:
Nicolaus Copernicus
Mahatma Gandhi
Edgar Allan Poe
Indira Gandhi
Cecil B. De Mille
Pablo Picasso
Howard Hughes
Jacqueline Kennedy Onassis
Princess Grace of Monaco
Barbara Walters
Muhammad Ali
Oprah Winfrey
Bob Dylan
Sarah Jessica Parker
Bernie Sanders,
Robert Downey, Jr.

The 7th animal is the HORSE

High noon is ruled by the Horse (11 am to 1 pm).

The horse leads the way to the barnyard animals that rule the p.m. hours. We know the barnyard; it's familiar. The Horse leads the pack and the parade. The Horse is very visible, and is an animal that people love.

Just as people are afraid of Rats, they will see the Horses, the opposite sign, as wonderful. They symbolize all the power and graciousness in the parade.

Horses are made to lead. Even if their ideas are not the most exceptional, their leadership qualities are. A good example of a Horse would be FDR—our 32nd President of the United States, Franklin Delanor Roosevelt. He was a good Horse. We won't be able to say what especially he did that was so brilliant, but he took charge of a world that was incapacitated and the rest of us allowed him to lead us.

Other Famous Horses include:

Neil Armstrong, Sean Connery, Clint Eastwood, Harrison Ford, Barbara Streisand, Kevin Costner, Michael Crichton, Robert Duvall, Denzel Washington, Vladimir Ilyich Lenin, Thomas Edison, Theodore Roosevelt, the Duke of Windsor, Boris N. Yeltsin, Leonid Brezhnev, Anwar Sadat, Nelson Mandela, J. Edgar Hoover, Warren Buffet, Joanne Woodward, and Paul McCartney.

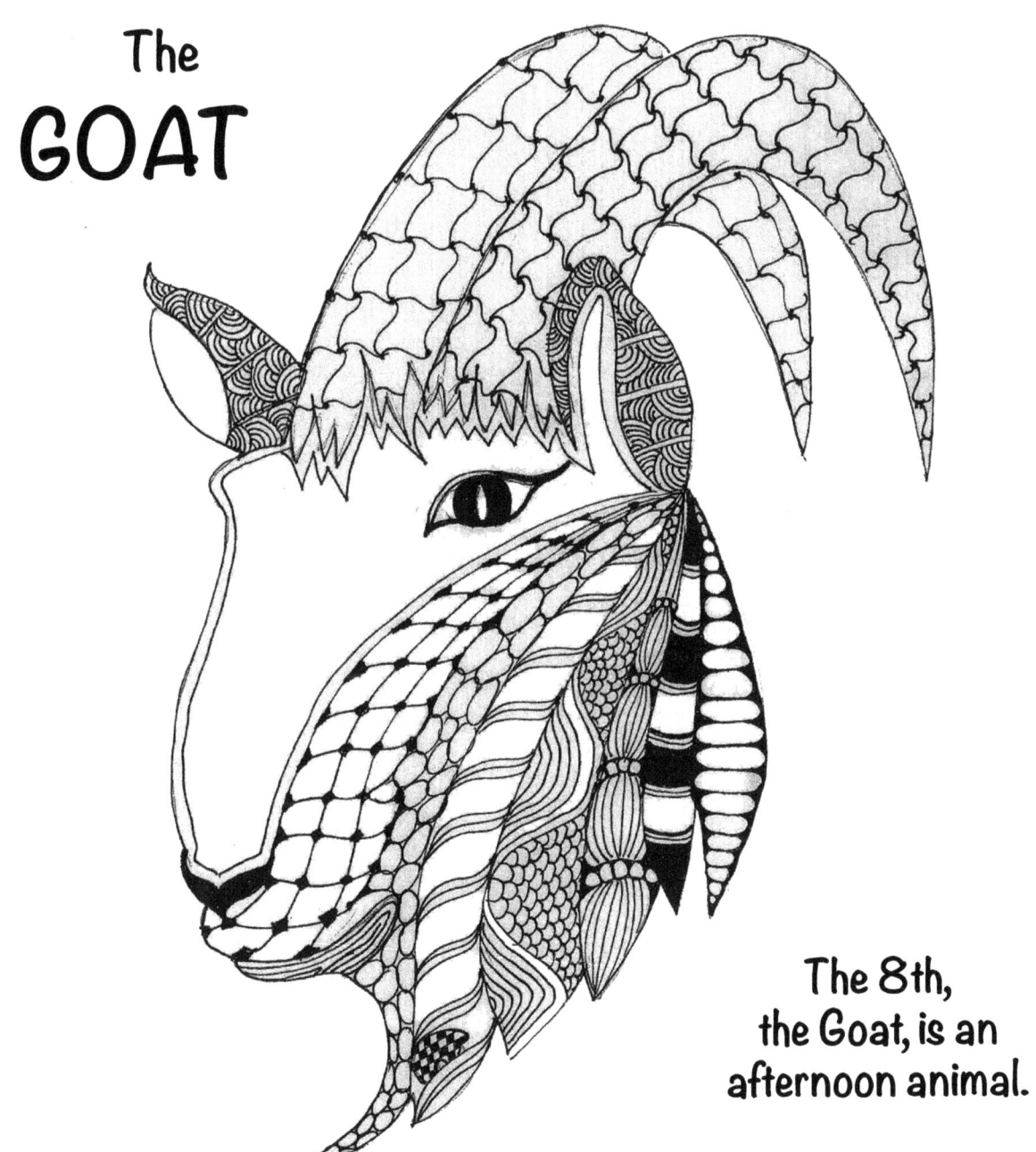

The GOAT

The 8th, the Goat, is an afternoon animal.

(1 - 3 pm).

The Goat, the 8th animal, is the most artistic of the 12 animals, whether it is drawing, poetry, writing, photography, or blowing glass.

Goats can get along well with everybody.

There is a saying in Chinese astrology that if you want to have a successful dinner party, invite a Goat because they are always enchanting.

Hardworking animals like the Ox may not appreciate the Goat because goats get by with a lot of perks. They are, after all, charming, cute, artistic, playful, and creative.

Goats don't usually have a strong need to lead—instead they enjoy being a member of the team.

Famous Goats include:
Michelangelo, Benito Mussolini,
Rudolph Valentino, Mark Twain, Babe Ruth,
John Wayne, Mikhail Gorbachev, Ben Kingsley,
Dan Rather, George Harrison, Mick Jagger,
Robert DeNiro, Phillip Seymour Hoffman,
Whoopi Goldberg, Bruce Willis, Julia Roberts,
Steve Jobs, Bill Gates.

The MONKEY

The 9th, the Monkey is the most human-like of all the animals in the Chinese Zodiac (3 - 5 pm).

Monkeys are very smart and capable of doing anything. They excel at leadership, writing, business—everything and anything.

When I see a biography or an obituary that includes about 15 different occupations in a lifetime, I know that person was born in the Year of the Monkey!

Monkeys are brainy and courageous with the ability to deal with almost all life situations comfortably--except love. This is their short suit. They understand how things work, but they don't know what happens in the irrational realm. They think you can run a love affair like a business plan. It can't be done.

Famous Monkeys include:
Leonardo Da Vinci, Marquis de Sade,
Paul Gauguin, Charles Dickens, Eleanor Roosevelt,
Harry S. Truman, F. Scott Fitzgerald,
Nelson Rockefeller, Elizabeth Taylor,
Danny De Vito, Edward M. Kennedy,
Katie Couric, Will Smith,
and Tom Hanks

The ROOSTER

The 10th, the Rooster straddles night and day on the Western side (5 - 7 pm).

Roosters are always pecking and never rest. Very hardworking animals, they frequently work much harder than the compensation they receive.

The size of the animal often has to do with the intellectual capacity. It is not that big animals are dumb and small animals are smart. It is just that big animals don't have to depend so much on their brain as small animals do.

For example, the Rat, Snake, and Rooster are the most intellectually capable animals because they have to use their mental power to protect themselves and survive in the world where there are larger, powerful creatures that may hurt them.

The Rooster is relentless, with an inner ambition, but often may have difficulty in achieving the high recognition that work often merits. Roosters like to wear uniforms that tell you who they are. If they are not in a military role, the Rooster will wear clothing with status.

Famous Roosters include:

Benjamin Franklin, William Faulkner, Errol Flynn, General George S. Patton, Katharine Hepburn, Joan Rivers, Michael Caine, Carol Burnett, Bette Midler, Dolly Parton, Elton John, Diane Keaton, Jennifer Lopez, and Beyoncé Knowles.

The
DOG

The 11th, the Dog
is born to serve
(7 - 9 pm).

Dogs are honest, intelligent, and straightforward with a deep sense of loyalty and passion for justice.

Dogs may be the most honored sign in the Chinese Zodiac. They are born to serve their master and their household. This humanitarian protects the people who are there.

Dogs are inclined to bark if they sense danger and their bark usually equates to sharp words.

Not everybody likes to be with the Dog because dogs can have sharp tongues. They don't spare their comments and can be cynical. If Dogs don't like something, they will speak up.

Famous Dogs include:

Sir Winston Churchill, Bertold Brecht, Harry Houdini,
John D. Rockefeller, Golda Meir, Mother Theresa,
Elvis Presley, Ralph Nader, Donald Trump, William J. Clinton, Cher,
Susan Sarandon, Madonna, Michael Jackson, Sylvester Stallone,
Sally Field, Steven Spielberg, Andre Agassi

The PIG

The 12th, the Pig completes the Chinese Zodiac (9 - 11 pm).

The Pig is considered to be one of the most fortunate of the animals because everything seems to go his way. Pigs are fortunate because they make money, and they enjoy keeping connected with people.

The Asian people have roast Pig for their celebration of the Chinese New Year. Therefore, the Pig must be fattened, and must not be stressed or endangered in any way, so they can have the perfect Pig for the feast.

People of the sign of the Pig are considered to be generous regarding possessions. They will give you the coat off their back if you need it, but will also take anything you have if they need it. Pigs don't really see boundaries. They are comfortable in communal situations where they share. The Pig is not a sign that worries a lot. Things seem to go well with them, so they feel secure about the future. They are honest, sympathetic, simple, and courageous.

Pigs like to talk a lot. They are very smart animals who like to tell you whatever they know. A good example of a Pig is Henry Kissinger, Nixon's Secretary of State. As a professor at Harvard, he never stopped talking and still gives speeches today about any ongoing world event.

Other famous Pigs include:

Henry VIII of England, Otto Von Bismarck (Prince of Bismarck), John D. Rockefeller, Ernest Hemingway, Vladimir Nabokov, Alfred Hitchcock, Ronald Reagan, O J Simpson, Hillary Rodham Clinton, Arnold Schwarzenegger, Stephen King, Camilla Parker Bowles, Billy Crystal, Kevin Kline, Kevin Spacey, Richard Dreyfuss, Lance Armstrong.

WHAT NEXT?

So, what should you do with this new found knowledge?

How do you integrate this information into your existing study of Astrology?

Two of the most important characteristics of an astrologer would be observation and experience. Determine which animals surround you within your family and your friends.

Observe their behavior and note if it corresponds to how you feel about that animal. Is that a characteristic that you would associate with a Snake? Does this person seem to have the energy of an Ox?

Take the time to observe the world you occupy and feel these animals. Your experience of the energy of those around you will tell you what characteristics they have in common with each of these animals. Use that information as an adjunct to your study of Western Astrology.

Enjoy the fascinating and the unique energy of each of the animals of Chinese Astrology and then modify your understanding of western charts by adding the color of these Animals!

THE CHINESE CALENDAR, 1937-2020 (Fire Ox to Metal Rat)

Year	sign	element	year begins
1937	Ox	fire	2/11
1938	Tiger	earth	1/31
1939	Rabbit	earth	2/19
1940	Dragon	metal	2/8
1941	Snake	metal	1/27
1942	Horse	water	2/15
1943	Goat	water	2/05
1944	Monkey	wood	1/25
1945	Rooster	wood	2/13
1946	Dog	fire	2/2
1947	Pig	fire	1/22
1948	Rat	earth	2/10
1949	Ox	earth	1/29
1950	Tiger	metal	2/17
1951	Rabbit	metal	2/6
1952	Dragon	water	1/27
1953	Snake	water	2/14
1954	Horse	wood	2/3
1955	Goat	wood	1/24
1956	Monkey	fire	2/9
1957	Rooster	fire	1/31
1958	Dog	metal	2/18
1959	Pig	fire	2/8
1960	Rat	metal	1/28
1961	Ox	metal	2/15
1962	Tiger	water	2/5
1963	Rabbit	water	1/25
1964	Dragon	wood	2/13

Year	sign	element	year begins
1965	Snake	wood	2/2
1966	Horse	fire	1/21
1967	Goat	fire	2/9
1968	Monkey	earth	1/30
1969	Rooster	earth	2/17
1970	Dog	metal	2/6
1971	Pig	metal	1/27
1972	Rat	water	2/15
1973	Ox	water	2/3
1974	Tiger	wood	1/23
1975	Rabbit	wood	2/11
1976	Dragon	fire	1/31
1977	Snake	fire	2/18
1978	Horse	earth	2/7
1979	Goat	earth	1/28
1980	Monkey	metal	2/16
1981	Rooster	metal	2/5
1982	Dog	water	1/25
1983	Pig	water	2/13
1984	Rat	wood	2/2
1985	Ox	wood	2/20
1986	Tiger	fire	2/9
1987	Rabbit	fire	1/29
1988	Dragon	earth	2/17
1989	Snake	earth	2/6
1990	Horse	metal	1/27
1991	Goat	metal	2/15
1992	Monkey	water	2/4
1993	Rooster	water	1/23

Year	sign	element	year begins
1994	Dog	wood	2/10
1995	Pig	wood	1/31
1996	Rat	fire	2/19
1997	Ox	fire	2/7
1998	Tiger	earth	1/28
1999	Rabbit	earth	2/16
2000	Dragon	metal	2/5
2001	Snake	metal	1/24
2002	Horse	water	2/12
2003	Goat	water	2/01
2004	Monkey	wood	1/22
2005	Rooster	wood	2/9
2006	Dog	fire	1/29
2007	Pig	fire	2/18
2008	Rat	earth	2/7
2009	Ox	earth	1/26
2010	Tiger	metal	2/14
2011	Rabbit	metal	2/3
2012	Dragon	water	1/23
2013	Snake	water	2/10
2014	Horse	wood	1/31
2015	Goat	wood	2/19
2016	Monkey	fire	2/8
2017	Rooster	fire	1/28
2018	Dog	earth	2/16
2019	Pig	earth	2/5
2020	Rat	metal	1/25

http://www.chinese-astrology.co.uk/rat.html

A Special Offer—Now that you know your animal sign, would you like to have a picture of it, in an 11 inch x 14 inch art mat, all ready to place into a frame?

$24.95 each plus postage.

Here are two examples. The choice of horizontal or vertical will be selected according to which is best to display the drawing, its title and the date of birth.

If you would like the print to also include your name, (or the name of the recipient, if you intend it as a gift), be sure to state the name exactly as you want it to appear (first name only or entire name), when you place your order.

Since these prints are personalized, they are not returnable. Each print will be in an art mat with a clear protective sleeve. Remove the sleeve before placing the matted print into a frame with glass.

To Order, call 603-734-4300 M-F, 10am-3pm ET, or order online at www.astrocom.com

About the Author
Monica Hable Dimino

Monica, BSN, is a full time consulting astrologer with a large international clientele. She was born in Wisconsin, did post graduate studies in education at NYU, taught pediatric nursing at Belleville School of Nursing until marriage in 1958, then moved to Caracas, Venezuila with her husband. It was there that she "discovered" astrology.

Monica writes: "Tossed into this multilingual world, I combed French and Spanish bookstores for reading material to support my study of languages. One fine day in 1959, I picked up a book by Andre Barbault, a famous French astrologer, which was a real page turner. That was it! Then, a French speaking friend gave me a gift that has been a companion to my astrological studies for over 50 years. It was Paula Delsol's "Horoscopes Chinois."

"I lived in Caracas for 30 years, most of them totally immersed in astrology. To help me in the field of consulting, I enrolled in a three year program to become a certified Gestalt Therapist in 1980. In 1988, I left "les beaux tropiques" and returned to the United States. Since then, I've been teaching, writing and consulting ... always with astrology as the vital force."

Monica, a mother of four, currently resides with her husband, Michael, in Watertown, Massachusetts.

About the Co-Author and Illustrator
Paula Sherwin

Paula, as co-author and the illustrator of this book, was born and raised in Utah. She earned her Master of Education degree from Utah State University, and has been a technical instructor in high tech companies such as EMC, Motorola and Wang Labs for 20 years.

Paula has been a certified Zentangle trainer for five years. She also has an active career as a practicing astrologer, and has a website on which her services can be seen as Paula, The Astro Lady (www.paulatheastrolady.com)

The beautiful zentangle animal drawings that illustrate this book were drawn by Paula, and she also created the full color zentangle design that is shown on the cover. Paula says that the Zentangle® Method is an easy-to-learn, relaxing, and fun way to create beautiful images by drawing structured patterns. It was created by Rick Roberts and Maria Thomas.

"Zentangle" is a registered trademark of Zentangle, Inc. and more can be learned about it at their website: **www.zentangle.com.**

Currently Paula lives in New England with her two daughters, Alexis and Sierra Sherwin. This is her first book.

Personalized Astrology Lessons

A special course in basic astrology that teaches you with examples from your own personal horoscope!

Maritha Pottenger created these unique personalized lessons to assist beginners in understanding the tools that astrology has to offer.

With her activist approach to astrology, you are shown how to create your future, and achieve the life that you want!

Each lesson is reinforced with a special homework assignment that allows you to test yourself to see how well you've understood it.

Please specify the Lesson Numbers that you want when you place your order.

There are 32 lessons covering signs, houses, planets, elements and qualities, rulers, aspects, how to spot them and what they mean, then how to integrate all the separate parts of a horoscope. Lessons on "odds and ends, "such as the Moon's nodes, East Point and Vertex are included, too. You'll learn how to identify life areas in your horoscope, such as basic identity, career, mind and communication, relationships, parents, children, creativity and more—with each lesson using the one horoscope data—date, time and place—that you provide when you place your order. You can order all of the lessons at once, or a few at time, as you choose, at the prices show below, plus shipping.

All 32 lessons on one chart with the Notebook: PAL ALL-BOW 1 .... $99.95
One lesson, PAL-BOW1 .... $ 5.95   Notebook only NG-BOW1 .... $24.95
Any 6 lessons on 1 chart PAL6-BOW1...$24.95   Notebook only NB-BOW......$18.95

Astro Computing Services
Starcrafts LLC, 68 Fogg Rd, Epping NH 03042

www.astrocom.com
Phone orders: 603-734-4300 03042

Here is a classic 6-book course about how to learn astrology!
Popular and recommended by many for years!

You'll learn about all the basics of natal astrology—how to analyze and understand, how to look ahead, how to compare charts for relationship potential and how to answer questions! Astrologers over generations have learned from these two master teachers:

Marion D. March and Joan McEvers
Each book is $15.95

Book 1—Basic Principles
Learn the basics we all must learn when we begin: the planets, the signs, the houses and the aspects

Book 2—Basic Principles
Learn the basics we all must learn when we begin: the planets, the signs, the houses and the aspects

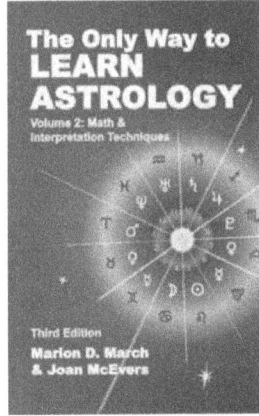

Book 3—Basic Principles
Learn the basics we all must learn when we begin: the planets, the signs, the houses and the aspects

Book 4—Basic Principles
Learn the basics we all must learn when we begin: the planets, the signs, the houses and the aspects

Book 5—Basic Principles
Learn the basics we all must learn when we begin: the planets, the signs, the houses and the aspects

Book 5—Basic Principles
Learn the basics we all must learn when we begin: the planets, the signs, the houses and the aspects

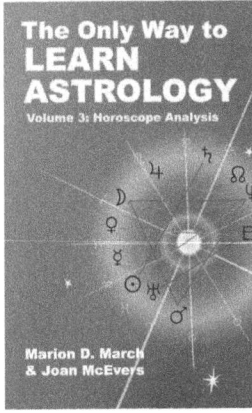

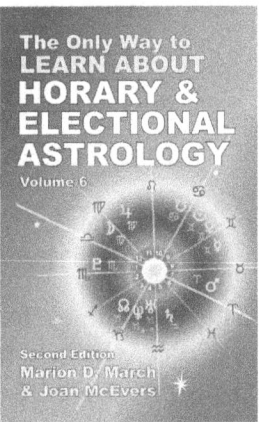

It's the ONLY WAY!

Starcrafts LLC  **Astro Computing Services** **ACS Publications**

Take a walk through United States history in an especially interesting way with this unique book based on Eris, the new planet discovered beyond Pluto in 2006, and then named for a Greek Goddess of Discord. Why???

Her discovery sent astronomers into turmoil, challenged Pluto, causing his demotion to "dwarf," now "minor" planet, thus upsetting the known solar system.

Who is Eris? And what does is she mean for we who are astrologers? This book has answers! You'll find 47 charts from USA history, events of upheaval and change, with stories and anecdotes about how the as yet unknown Eris was always "in play," within the charts!

Especially interesting is Tom Canfield's discovery of the "Frenemy Principle"—how Eris turns traditional aspect theory topsy-turvy. See how it works in charts! Also—Eris positions are listed yearly 1700-2050!   **$15.95**

When you change your place of residence, you change your horoscope!

With *Planets on the the Move*, you will:

- Discover the meaning and importance of aspects to the angles of your chart!
- Understand how changes of location can reflect in your experience of your chart!
- 49 charts are shown and interpreted to show you how relocation astrology works!

This is an important and well written book on relocation astrology by two famous authors! If you are now living in a different area from your birth, or are comtemplating a move, you'll want to read it!   **$16.95**

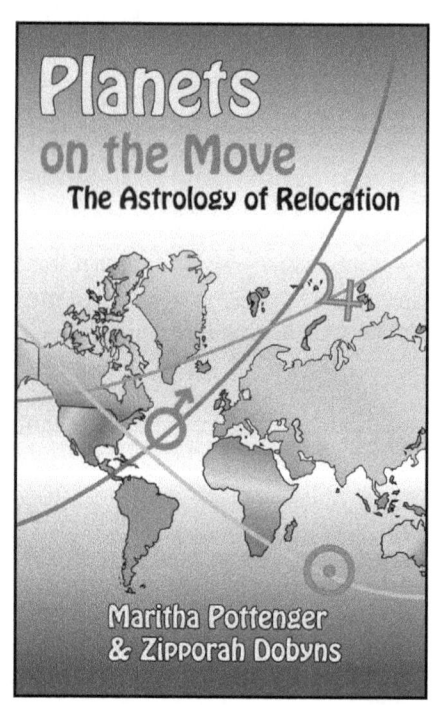

www.ingramcontent.com/pod-product-compliance
Ingram Content Group UK Ltd.
Pitfield, Milton Keynes, MK11 3LW, UK
UKHW050724100226
10596UKWH00075B/624